KEPT MOMENTS

KEPT MOMENTS

Gerhard E. Frost

WINSTON PRESS

Photographs by: Ed Cooper, pages x, 6, 16, and Paul
Conklin, pages 28, 40, 50, 58, 66, 80

Cover photo by Robert Friedman

"Intruder," "Disguise" (originally "Halloween Party"),
"Nativity," "Reverie," "The Face," and "The Story" are
reprinted from PARISH TEACHER, copyright 1981, by
permission of Augsburg Publishing House. "Side by Side"
(originally "It's Beautiful"), "Kept Moments," "Truth Must
Come In Person," and "Joy Over One" are reprinted from
PARISH TEACHER, copyright 1980, by permission of
Augsburg Publishing House.

All biblical quotations are from the *Revised Standard
Version of the Bible,* copyrighted 1946, 1952, 1971, 1973,
unless otherwise noted.

Library of Congress Catalog Card Number: 81-70844
ISBN: 0-86683-668-3
Printed in the United States of America.

5 4 3 2

Winston Press, Inc.
430 Oak Grove
Minneapolis, MN 55403

CONTENTS

Preface

Some books hold us. When we pick them up we can't lay them down but must read them to the end. They are meant to be devoured.

Other books are for nibbling. They don't hold us. They send us. We don't read them at a sitting. We find them slipping from limp hands and lying on our laps, not from drowsiness or boredom, but because we are sent on the wings of memory and imagination to our own private treasure house. We feel quietly alive, in need of nourishing and creative reverie.

Moments, whether winged with joy or heavy-footed with pain, are devoid of triteness. As gifts of God each is divinely innovative and full of possibility. But when considered qualitatively, some are more significant than others and deserve to live again and again in reminiscence and reflection. They are meant to be kept.

I hope that, to some small degree, this book will draw you in, then send you on your own most private excursions, to return in your own good time to read again.

Gerhard E. Frost
St. Paul, Minnesota

I REMEMBER

But when the time had fully come,
God sent forth his Son.

Galatians 4:4

I remember helping
when I was very little,
helping two chicks
out of their shells.
They both died.

I remember helping a rose to bloom;
it withered.

I remember pulling carrots
to see if they were ready,
then putting them back to grow.
They didn't.

I remember how hard it was to wait
for the fullness of time;
it still is.

But time always moves toward fullness;
it won't be hurried or held back;
it is God's very own creation
and all belongs to Him.

And that is good!

WHAT CAN I SAY?

We waited in the airport
and watched preliminary things,
tasting the pleasure
of anticipation, myself and others,
among them a man and a child.

I willingly overheard
their affectionate conversation
as question tumbled over question.
The crew arrived, uniformed,
smart and trim, co-pilot, flight
    attendants,
and now the pilot.

From child to father
the question came:
"Is that the driver?"
A nod was the response.
"Do you know him?"
The father shook his head.

Great God and Father,
author of life, my captain
and my crew, what can I say
when, one by one, the children ask,
"Do you know him?"

In Christ I see your face
and say my glad and grateful
"Yes!"

3

WE HAVE

We were speaking of children
and he shared this with me:

Little sisters, four and six;
today the mail brought
what they liked and looked for,
a catalogue, replete with
many colored pictures.

The first to page it
was the six year old;
she turned each page possessively,
saying wherever she found what
    pleased her,
"I want this! And I want this...and this!"

The ceremony of selfishness ended;
it was the moment of the four year old.
She, who didn't know the why of
    catalogues,
turned pages, pointing, too,
but now the words were new:
"We got this! And we got this...and this!"

"I want!" "We have!" What difference
it would make in this, our global village,
if four-year-old love and wisdom ruled
    the day!

DISGUISE

Someone said that it requires much
   courage
to walk into a room full
of human beings and be human.

I am reminded of a Halloween party
we had missed.

"How was the party?" we asked
of one who'd been there.
"Oh, fine," he answered,
"everyone came masked
and dressed like someone else,
and then there was a Saint Bernard;
he came as a dog."

Noble beast;
no mask, no wall,
no camouflage.
He came as himself.
To him the prize!

GOD AT WORK

Men at work the street sign says;
all traffic turns aside in deference.

Now it is May,
and all things green and earth-loved say
God at work.

What human hands can do has now been
    done;
the world awaits the miracle.
The farmer knows, has learned so well
that once the seed has found its place
he works by disciplined indifference,
by self-restraint and planned neglect.

The lesson?
Never molest a miracle
or kill by misspent industry
and over-help.

Is it so with those we love, but cannot
    lead?
Perhaps it is our greatest work to leave
    them
all alone in unmolested hiddenness,
to read the signals and believe the signs:
God at work.

LOST

"And how do the sheep get lost?"
the city dweller asked.
"Oh, they just put their heads down
and nibble themselves lost,"
the friendly shepherd said.

My Lord, it's now past noon,
and I've nibbled my way
from trivia to trivia
and don't know where I am.
Have mercy, redeem this heads-down day,
and put me on the trail again.

THE DIFFERENCE

He'd just received a box of crayons,
a birthday gift. Deluxe, it was,
with more than seventy colors,
and he was proud.

Whenever he found an audience
he'd empty every crayon out,
then separate the color families,
extolling the beauties of each.
Once, when the process ended,
he surprised a viewer
by reaching for one special crayon—
the periwinkle blue—
and saying, as he held it high,
"And this one is so pretty
it makes my eyes wet!"

He didn't say, "It makes me cry."
Young as he was, he knew the difference
between grief and encounter with
    transcendence.

What readiness to be touched by the
    intangible,
what openness to beauty and to God.

ALL MUST FALL

We sat on the bank,
high above the beautiful lake,
my beloved and I.

It was August,
and one leaf fell,
just one,
but as it fell,
it spoke.

We thought we heard it say,
"All leaves must fall,
come September and October.
All must fall."

It is far past August
in our life together—
at least November.

Dear Lord of falling leaves,
of far-spent days and flowing rivers,
help us, your frail and fragile ones,
to look serenely into the sunset glory
of this, your given day.

FAMILY TALK

It takes the whole church
to say "Jesus,"
and when all have said it,
you in your way
and I in mine,
what do we have?
Orchestrated understatement.

Our best dogma
of spoken creed
or faithful deed
is but the insufficient
baby talk of us,
the family of God.

Yet, He,
our Father,
takes pleasure,
and listens patiently
to our lisping growth.

LONGINGS

He's eighty-eight
and lives alone,
his every word a sea breeze
from "Sveden," his childhood home.

Yesterday I asked,
"Frank, are there times when you are
  lonely?"
"Aa ja, it comes and goes,"
was his ready reply.

Eight or eighty-eight,
it comes to all of us,
this mood of alienation,
it comes but also goes.

Where does it come from,
this bone-deep feeling
and sense of separation
that makes us strangers
in a hostile world?

Lord, you know.
Is my mood a summons from you,
an invitation and command
to call me home?
And where does it go?

Thank you for loneliness,
sent to tell me that this world
is not my home, nor can it ever be.

✹✹✹

NO REGRET

In the long catalogue of regrets,
one I've never heard
and don't expect to hear:
a dying person saying,
"If only I hadn't given so much!"

SIDE BY SIDE

Teaching is meeting on a bridge,
wide enough for two or more
to walk abreast together.

If I don't think I've much to learn
from one whom I'm about to teach,
I will but maim and insult—
it's better not to try.

Respect involves one in response,
shared struggle and excitement
on a bridge and crossing over
side by side.

THE THREAT

"And I'll skip you
in my prayers!"

The years have flown
since I overheard that tearful threat
from one who couldn't match
five years against the strength
and cunning of his older sibling.

Now there is the empty nest,
and I reflect on what that outcry meant:
a last resort, a final stand.
And now he is a man.

How large his world today,
how raw and sharp its edges.
Does he, I ask myself, now count prayer
as something to be treasured,
ultimate and priceless,
and will he always?

I bow my head.

REVERIE

There are times
for doing nothing,
but be sure you do it well—

and listen.

For God,
in silent spaces,
has something great
to tell.

A LIFE TO SHARE

He is my friend,
warm, magnanimous, and wise.
I heard him speak to students,
and this is what he said:

Give yourself to God in trust
and to your neighbor in love.
Remember, contempt for persons
besets us all. Servanthood centers
in grace and in our fellow humans.
We have a way of life to share;
if we're too busy for people,
we're busier than God.

Wherever you live, be sure to unpack;
no place on God's great earth
is just a stepping-stone.
People, profound and complex,
are always there, great as saints
and great as sinners. Be ready to forgive
and be forgiven.

Avoid the tyranny of swift success,
recalling that where persons are at stake
many things must just be lived with
    in love
and left undone,
awaiting the miracle of God.

IT COULD NOT BE

But God raised him to life again,
setting him free... because it could not be
that death should keep him in its grip.

Acts 2:24 NEB

Lord, it could not be
that death could hold him,
hold him or me.

That sets me free.

Death's grip is strong;
your grip is stronger still.
Help me to know the thing that cannot be.

THE INVITATION

Thank God
my Father's business
isn't busyness.

Today I prayed the "Our Father"
and he didn't interrupt to say,
"O.K., but make it short;
this is my busy day!"

He invited me
to stay.

SMALL TALK

"Granddaddy,
how did you marry grandma?"
"Oh, I became acquainted with her
and I loved her right away."
"Was she pretty?"
"Oh, yes!"

"Did she have light hair?"
"No, very, very dark. And she was
    graceful.
But, Rachel, you are pretty, too,
and you are graceful."
"Granddaddy, you don't have to
    say that."
"I know I don't."
"You don't have to say it for my feelings."
"I know. I wouldn't say it
if it weren't true."

The child probes, tests, checks,
already searching for integrity and honesty
in society's tangle of flattery and lies.

Small talk?
Who could call it that?

FAMILY

I heard it today—
that song: "There's nobody else
like you, nobody else, nobody else...."

Who am I?
One of God's originals,
unduplicated and unique.

One of me is all there is.

No one in this multi-colored, multi-lingual,
multi-everything mass of persons
combines the same characteristics
and capacities as I. That's why
there is no mass where persons are
    concerned—
no mass, only family.

No one is intended to play the same note.
I'm needed in the family orchestra.
I count because God counts me.

One Body in Christ;
I find myself in a relationship to you.
Like spokes in a wheel, the closer I am
to the center, the closer I am to you.

Harmony, coordination, concentration—
these are gifts I can bring. And what
are their other side?
Love, respect, and appreciation—
the spirit that makes music
in the family orchestra of God.

∿∿∿

PILGRIM

Why is a question so often best answered
with another question?

Is it because we are called and equipped
for journeying and that each horizon
beckons toward another?

TRIFLINGS

I sometimes wonder about the last
    moment
of that last, last day.

Will the power fail, the computers jam,
the switchboards close, the plumbing
    clog,
with no hot water for the baths?

Will I misplace my car keys,
forget the grocery list,
and will the carrier forget the letter
stamped three times: *Urgent!*?

I suppose.
But who will really notice?

THE CHALLENGE

"You shouldn't have come today,
because now you are the people
who know."

I felt singled out that day,
twenty-five years ago. I still do.

We had assembled in a new science
    facility
to dedicate and enjoy and to listen
to a scholar in the field of genetics,
and those were his closing words.
Bracing, compelling, personal—
the words still fill me
with the peril and promise
of things known and understood.

Closing words that day, but opening, too,
for they are a challenge, a reminder
that all new knowledge involves one
in greater responsibility and urgent
    choices.

THE CUP

Yes, Father, it does run over,
it really does. The cup, I mean.
But God, I didn't know, I couldn't guess
how big the cup would be,
how much of pain, but more of joy,
it someday would contain.

I'm glad today, and thankful, too,
for that early blindness. For had I seen
what fills it to the brim,
I would have spurned the cup;
I wouldn't have dared touch cup to lip.

I offer now my tear-stained praise.

FRAGRANT SYMBOLS

Thank you, God, for one year olds,
the turned-on ones—for Jennifer,
brightness and beauty in my days.

Today, while our tiny neighbor,
her mother, and I enjoyed the newly
   planted
petunias and marigolds, she reached
with eager confidence to gather a
   bouquet.

While every voice within her said,
"Look, Jennifer, smell, touch, enjoy!"
we startled her with the ancient,
   killjoy cry,
"Don't. Don't touch; don't pick!"

Arrested by the flashing signal
in the path of infant eagerness,
she turned. To what? That totally
touchable, pickable children's friend—
the dandelion.

Yes, thank you, God,
for Jennifer and for dandelions,
free, fantastic, fragrant symbols
of your inexhaustible grace.

FOOTNOTE

Why are people kinder, more human,
less critical and defensive,
more open to themselves and one
    another
before a crackling fire,
beside a flowing stream,
or under falling snow?
Why are we at our best
when looking at the stars
or walking in the rain?

Why is there therapy in sharing
the many moods of nature? I don't know,
but I have found it so.

Can it be that we are wrapped
in the blanket of creation more closely
than we know?

Does our great Father-Creator speak
through these many voices to reach us,
one by one?

And is it one grand footnote
to Christ, the Word, sent as Person
to seek and save us all?

29

THE LESSON

She teaches little children
the rudiments of art;
today they worked with watercolors.

The session ended, one gifted child
presented his finished masterpiece.
Kindly, and with great appreciation,
she responded,
then added two careful brush strokes
to fill it in a bit.

Instantly, a small hand took the picture,
and tearing it from top to bottom,
the little artist said,
"If anybody's going to spoil this, I am!"

He learned a lesson, but she,
the teacher, learned one, too:
respect for rights of ownership,
the sacred turf of the creator.
How different help may look
when seen through others' eyes,
and how important for grown-ups
to walk in little shoes!

BUT WE HAD HOPED

*But we had hoped
that he was the one....*

Luke 24:21

When faith slips
and slides into
the past tense,
when alleluias turn
to postmortems
and all appears
to be lost;
then, thank God,
he is known in
the breaking of bread.

DIMINISHED

He died today;
they sat him down alone,
alone in that cold chair,
strapped him to hopelessness
and dark despair.

Five men took aim.
They couldn't miss
and didn't.

We grope and fumble for a word,
and call it justice,
but are not satisfied.

Defeat, dead end for all of us,
mocks and shames, convicts, embarrasses,
leaves only leaden silence.

I look at you; you look at me.
We look away.

He died today; I am diminished,
and all humans with me. Have mercy,
    Lord,
on him, on me, on us, the sinners.

LOOK AGAIN

If you would live creatively,
look again at what God
has placed before you
but you have never fully seen:
a place, a situation, an idea,
a person, a face—especially the face
of one you love or hate,
of one you take for granted or ignore,
or one prejudged and now avoided.

There never was a human face
that wasn't worth another look.

LIFE IS LIKE THAT

Her first recital night,
so she was "artiste-in-the-wings"
as she promenaded in her gown,
ankle length.

It was early, just six-thirty,
when we came to pick her up,
but they were to be there
to try the big, black Steinway
and become a bit accustomed.

A long evening it would be,
and a nervous one,
so as she approached,
flushed and radiant,
we whispered to each other
things mundane but necessary.
We hesitated to mar her sense of
    occasion,
but life is like that, so we asked:
"Have you been to the bathroom?"
Grudgingly the answer came: "No."
"Don't you have to go?"
Again, more grudging still,
"Not *very* bad."

It's hard to face reality,
dressed for a dream.

ENCOUNTER

I walked today where Jesus walked.
I didn't meet a number
or smile at a statistic
or laugh with a cipher.

I didn't talk about the weather
or swap a story
or exchange a handclasp with a case,
a client, or a keypunch in a computer card.

I met people, persons like you and me
and Jesus.

Yes, I kept meeting Jesus;
the streets were full of him.

BENEDICTION

Preschool,
and she didn't like it.
Standing in the shadows of the
     cloakroom,
I sadly helped her with her overshoes
as the bell began to ring.

With only seconds to think,
my mind stumbled and raced:
"What can I say? Is there no word,
     O God?
Give me one thought to anchor a day,
to comfort this child and chase a tear
     away!"

It came:
"You are blessed, little one;
remember, Granddaddy told you,
you are blessed!"

A quick caress, and she was away,
no, not quite, for just as she was about
to step beyond my view, she turned,
and with a smile, she said,
"And *you* are blessed."

Of all the times
I've received the blessing,
alone or with many others,
I remember best the benediction
that ricocheted back to me
from the heart of a smiling
child.

❧❧❧

A WORLD BEYOND

If you treasure insight,
don't scorn the hard and painful moment;
remember that your tears are
sometimes telescopes.

EVERY GOOD GIFT

... Every good gift and every perfect gift is from above, and cometh down from the Father of lights. ...

James 1:17 KJV

Face to face
we rocked and talked,
her short legs straddling me,
experiencing contentment,
man and child.

Suddenly she exclaimed
to my surprise, "I'm rocking you!"
"No, really," I replied. "I'm rocking you.
I'm the one whose feet can touch the
    floor.
When I push gently, I rock us both
back and forth, back and forth."

I've smiled at her mistake and thought,
"Isn't this the one we grown-ups make?"
There's only one who holds and rocks
his world in his unfailing care;
in him alone is love.

PROMISE

April, and promise filled the air.
We sat beneath the oak trees,
retreating together and talking.
The subject: the right to live—
even when the road is uphill all the way
and only suffering seems to lie ahead.

One among us hadn't spoken.
Now he did—slowly, softly,
every word a painful effort:
"We mustn't deprive them
of the process," was all he said.

Did he mean that living,
even in its bleakest moment,
holds promise, promise like
an April morning?

Words to search and silence us.

WORDS TO THE YOUNG

Remember,
life is God-sized,
his gift to give.
Never trivialize it
by paring down its questions.
Let Truth be as unruly as it is;
let it carry you where you dare not go
and where, today, you fear to be.

Strive to know—
that is a noble dedication—
but in all your knowing, remember
you may be tempted to shrink your
    world
to what you know and slowly cease to
    catch your breath
in awe and wonder.

Never disdain or underestimate
those gifts that God wraps in the
    everyday;
he has no need to over-dress his
    benedictions;
his small and daily blessings are the strong
    threads
that bind the tapestry of life together.

KEPT MOMENTS

And his mother kept all these things
in her heart.

Luke 2:51

A disturbing experience
for Mary and Joseph:
losing their boy for three days,
then finding him in the Temple,
listening and asking,
surprised that they were worried.

An unsettling event,
leaving much to think about,
so Mary did what mothers do so well:
she kept all these things;
stored them in her heart.

Our hearts have ample room
for keeping thoughts
that tell us who we are
and make us what we are becoming.

INSIGHT

Yesterday at dusk
we drove the city freeway,
and she exclaimed, "Oh, look!
Isn't that a beautiful sunset?
Just a little bit of heaven—
oh, no, of course not;
anything on earth compared with heaven
would be like an apple core
or an orange pit—do oranges have pits?"
"No, but prunes do."
"O.K., an apple core or a prune pit!"

Who but a child
could cut so deftly
through the crust of things
and intuitively sense the glory
to be revealed?

THE NAMED ONE

And Jacob was left alone;
and a man wrestled with him
until the breaking of the day...
and Jacob's thigh
was put out of joint....
Then he said, "Your name
shall no more be called Jacob,
but Israel...."

Genesis 32:24-28

"How are you today?" I enquired
of my slightly crippled friend.
"Oh, all right," he answered with a smile,
"but I still walk with a limp."
"Don't we all?" I said.

And I've been thinking—
this must be what our most shaping
God-meetings mean: To be named is
to be lamed. Abram is Abraham;
Jacob is Israel; Saul is Paul.
No one is the same.
Such is the mark of chastening love.

TRUTH MUST COME IN PERSON

The room was crowded,
the acoustics poor,
so as the speaker droned,
"When a child is indifferent or unruly,
it is usually best to switch his attention,"
a tired voice from the rear asked,
"Switch his what?"

But perhaps it is more than a matter
of switching the attention.
Truth must come in person
if it is to engage the will
and excite the imagination.

My friend says it well:
The ultimate sin against truth
is to bore people with it.

IT'S YOURS, LORD

Forever—
I say it to myself, Lord,
say it again and again.
It frightens me. I'm tormented,
haunted, and all but upended.
It robs me of all peace and rest.

Forever—
too long, too deep, too high,
too much, Lord;
I can't handle it.
You take it, please,
it's yours, all yours;
you hold it, and me,
in the hollow of your hand.

NEVER TOO BUSY

This morning, very early,
I sensed the Spirit stirring
at the latchstring of my heart.
"Good morning, may I come in?" he said,
and then he came.

We shared secrets,
mine of musty darkness,
his of blinding light.
We spoke of many things,
of this day and tomorrow,
of joy and pain, life and life again.

We spoke of death—
my death.

Feeling my heart's tremor,
he said, "You needn't hurry.
My world can wait."
At last I stammered softly,
"This is the best; may we do it again?"
"I'm never too busy," he said.

BOXED IN

She colored a giraffe today,
one ear pink, the other green,
a tail of blue, the body brown
with spots of many colors.

She brought her joyful offering
into the world of grown-ups,
and the first to see it said,
"But no one has ever seen
a giraffe like that!"
"Isn't that too bad!" was all she said.

Keep resisting, child,
those little boxes,
the cramped and stuffy judgments
that bury one alive.
Fight the brave battle
to be the one you are.

PARTNERS

When I think of teaching,
I reflect on two rules:
Know what you want to do
and how you'd like to do it,
and be prepared to do something else.

Comprehensive rules,
the second more difficult than the first
and equally important.

To bring a class a rigid lesson plan
is to demand response
without consenting to answer,
to say, "I'm excited, and I command you
to take my excitement as yours,
but do not offer me your own."

Education, like a tango,
takes two.

INTRUDER

She's not quite sixteen.
I spied her just this evening
on the dock, at sunset,
alone.

I didn't think;
I just barged in.
I didn't say,
"May I come in?"

I broke the spell.

Lord, I know
solitude is your
very special gift,
sometimes too great
to share with anyone.

I should have given
what was mine to give,
my absence, then.

GOOD SENSE

I saw him only once,
my traveling companion
on our way to Boston,
back in the railroad's glory days.
We were both young then;
not so today, but I remember him
for something that he said.

He was a ready talker
with not much room for silence.
For hours we moved from this to that
in easy-to-be-forgotten repartee,
but this, of all he said, remains with me:
"I always talk to old people."

If I could see him now
I'd thank him, and I'd say
how many times I've recalled,
and even practiced, what he said.
Good sense, to speak to those
who've been there, to listen
while they're here,
and not regret.

HE IS HERE

"They have no wine," Mary said,
and it was true, but there was more—
there was a guest—
Jesus was there.

Jesus is here,
in our lost festivity,
our wineless celebrations
and abortive, empty-eyed salutes
to boredom and despair.

Jesus inhabits our days.
We are the world he looks upon
and loves.

Expect a miracle, look to him;
he quenches thirst and fire—
and death!

LEARN OF ME

Take my yoke upon you,
and learn of me.

Matthew 11:29 KJV

But God, you don't follow my script;
it isn't my scenario; it isn't what I wrote.
Have you lost it?

I have to learn of you, you say?
Word for word, line for line?

I see! Forgive me, Lord,
for ever having had a script.
Make me a learner all my days.

THE QUESTION

Today, as we talked,
friend to friend,
she shared this memory with me.

Keeping vigil at her sister's side
with death only moments away,
she longed to share thought and feeling,
but the dear one had moved beyond,
out of reach as she lay
in comatose stillness.

Suddenly she stirred
and startled the waiting one
with a question, " 'Yea' what, Ethel?"
Some seconds of panic
("What does she mean? What does
she want? I mustn't fail her now!"),
and then as a gift, the answer came:
"Yea, though I walk through the valley
of the shadow of death, I will fear
no evil, for thou art with me."

The dying one smiled and said,
"I will fear no evil, for thou art
with me, with me..." and on this
she pillowed her head.

SMILE

Monday, Easter Monday—
to me, a long and wearying day,
and there it was again, that
sickening, sentimental word: *Smile!*
It seemed I'd read it on a hundred desks,
a thousand bumper stickers.

A command, of all things!

I raised my inner fists
in self-protective gesture
as I shouted to myself
and nobody in particular:
"Show me a reason! Don't you know
that joy can never be commanded?
I want a reason.
Don't ask me to be a phony
and a hypocrite."

Then it came.
It came from yesterday,
floating on a tiny current of memory:
"He is risen. He is not here. Hallelujah!"

I smiled an honest smile.

RECONCILER

He is small for his age,
this very special child,
and some would say he's
far behind.

It happened outside the dentist's office
in a small and crowded waiting room.

He was just himself,
unafraid to bring his gift of love.
He talked to one and then another,
brought them all together.

He broke down walls
and scattered love for all to share,
this one so far behind, and yet
so far ahead.

I heard it all from one who'd been there.
"There were no strangers left," she said.
"We felt as one together."

GOD BLESS

God bless the bright-eyed,
brash and buoyant one
who's always getting
into things.

In heaven they must say,
"What's he into now?"

Into a task too big for him,
into the feast and fun of life,
biting off more than he can chew,
into the Gift he plunges headlong,
trusting that it is meant for him.

KEEP ME RESTLESS

*We... look for new heavens
and a new earth....*

2 Peter 3:13 KJV

Hand in hand we walked and talked
as we climbed the winding stair
(she was only three)
in the big house.
I steadied each giant stride,
enjoying every moment.

"What are we doing?" she asked.
"Looking for my car keys," I replied.
"Oh, Granddaddy," she exclaimed,
"you're always looking for and
     looking for!"

"The story of my life," I said,
but only to myself;
she couldn't have understood.

But, Lord, you understand;
I'm yours, I'm of your searching clan,
at home away from home.
Lord, hold me, steady my faltering steps,
but keep me restless in my rest,
waiting, hoping, journeying,
"...always looking for and looking for."

PROMPTERS

Waiting at a bus stop
I tossed some crumbs into the city street.
With a whir of wings the pigeons came,
sixteen of them. I counted.

From where, I cannot tell,
but the dove is always there
in urban and in rural scene.

I've wondered, Why so many pigeons,
cluttering city pavements,
dusting on the country roads?
Are they God's special greeting to the
    poor?
his gifts to lonely persons,
companions in their empty days?

And are they Pentecost birds,
prompters of us, forgetful people,
lest we forget our lonely neighbor
and the Spirit, who, at the Savior's
    baptism,
descended like a dove?

ACCEPTANCE

I stood on a summit today
as I read John 17,
Christ's high-priestly prayer.
I knew he had left me far behind;
I felt shut out, but loved.

Like a tiny child I waited and wondered,
listened while our Savior prayed
for "them," for you and me, for us:
"Holy Father, keep them...
that they may have my joy fulfilled in
   them...
sanctify them in thy truth...
that they may all be one."

Memory carries me back
to the time when I was the littlest;
back to the chilly mornings
when I'd creep into my mother's bed
while father stirred the embers.
I'd lay my restless head on her soft arm,
but if her lips were moving and she didn't
look at me, I'd know that she was
   praying.
I wouldn't talk; I'd be so very still.
I felt shut out, but loved.

Shut out? No, never.
Not really, not rejected.
I knew that she was getting ready,
preparing for her day,
and that included me.
So also when our Savior prays.
We're in his day,
this day full of grace.
He prays for us, his loved ones,
and we are not shut out.

*

THANK GOD

In the "O God" moment,
the worst and best, the far out time,
when words are weak and language fails,
then, thank God for tears, for swift
    embrace
and touch and laughter—and silence!

PRAYER

Be still, and know that I am God.

Prayer?
What is it
but letting God be God,
letting him love you in your being
and in your becoming?

Prayer.
The stillness you know
when you wait because
you know who waits
for you.

THE FACE

Truth is the face
of a long-forgotten friend,
the one for whom we're made.
Therefore, in learning,
we say, "I see!"
and celebrate.

Learning is reunion,
joyful recognition
of the face, once known
(before we became a broken race),
the joy of two who are
meant for each other.

Truth is the face
of God.

PERFECTIONIST

Father, I hear them—
the eager ones,
slamming the door,
leaving for another day in school.

Help me today—
me, your slow learner in the School of
    Grace.
Help me, the accepted one,
though unacceptable,
to affirm them
and receive them
as they are.
Help me not to throw away this
    irretrievable moment
in smoothing, correcting, combing,
straightening, buttoning and unbuttoning.
Help me to see that life is more
than grammar, spelling, and posture.
Help me not to let the misspelled word
blind me to the rest of the page.
Amen.

CHASTENED

An unrelenting winter
(Will it never end, we said),
but then it came:
summer, 1979.

Awaited, but remembered, too,
for when it came it brought the
    inchworm,
hordes and armies, attacking leaf and bud,
leaving elm trees stripped and bare.

Then the unexpected happened;
the summer of the inchworm
became the special summer of the oriole
and robin, too.

With porch space for our box seats,
without ticket or permission
and no leafy visual obstruction,
we watched the nesting families,
rewarded by the classic beauty
and day-by-day drama of their lives.

How often we've been chastened
and sometimes all but broken
by the pesky inchworms of discouraging
    events,
yet found them yielding strength and beauty
to the late and ripening years.

JOY OVER ONE

I tell you there is joy
before the angels of God
over one sinner who repents.

Luke 15:10

Jesus said it, and he wants us to know:
there's a party in heaven
when a sinner repents.

Our Father is like that:
beautifully greedy on behalf of his family.
He wants all the children in.

We couldn't approach him
if his love didn't draw us;
we couldn't come in
if he didn't call.

God doesn't need us but he wants us all
in his place prepared.

HE'LL DO IT AGAIN

And suddenly a light
from heaven flashed about him.
And he fell to the ground
and heard a voice saying...
"Saul, Saul."

Acts 9:3-4

Saul, the proud one,
thought he owned the road;
when suddenly God's highway patrol
just flagged him down with blinding light,
and he was Paul, the little one.

He had an agenda, proud Saul did,
but this Jesus scrambled it;
he did it then, and he'll do it again.

Just when you've straightened your halo
and you're speeding down the great
    white way
to nowhere, God puts you on his
    cloverleaf,
makes you start right over again.
When you're so sincere (as Saul was)
and doing everything just right,
and God is all mixed up
with memories and mortgages,
television and Tuesdays,
graduations and graveyards;

when you're so religious,
so in touch and in tune,
and suddenly, at the count of one,
God's seeking love surfaces as devastating
    power,
then morning dew
becomes torrential rain,
and the gentle breath of God
a hurricane that blows away
your pride.

≈≈≈

DEFECTOR

If one can set aside one's faith
as casually as one sets down
a piece of luggage
and then walk away from it,
that's probably all it ever was.

CHILD WISDOM

I couldn't suppress a smile
when she, the ten year old,
shared a self-searching moment:
"I don't know what I'm going to do
with my life; there are so many things
I'm interested in, but I've already
invested ten years in art."

Today I thank that wistful child
who spoke more wisely than she knew.

God dreams his dream for me,
enlists me for the full-time task of
    moving on.
My life is a becoming;
he will not let me be.
There's no rehearsal for the art of living;
no vacation from the journeying.

It all begins with his first gift—
day one!

THE GOAL

In parenting and teaching,
let this be our aim:
not to make every idea
safe for children, but
every child safe
for ideas.

COMPANIONS

"Do you rest well,
or do the nights seem long?"
"Oh, I don't always sleep well,
and I awaken early almost every morning,
but I have such good times
with the Lord!"

My conversation
with a white-haired friend,
queen of ninety summers;
and it awakens memories.

I remember the delight of eavesdropping
at the threshold of our baby's room
many, many years ago; listening
to cooing and laughter over a shadow,
a sunbeam, a bit of lint on the tip
of a tiny finger—total absorption
in the endless surprise
of being alive.

Traveling companions—
one a new arrival
the other soon to depart—
united in wonderment,
exploration, and joy.

GLORY

*The heavenly guest
is at the door.*

The other day, at dawn,
for just a moment,
the lines were clear.

I saw.

Today they blur again,
but then, for a little while,
I saw, I really did.

And, thank God,
I'll see again.

A LESSON

Today I learned a lesson,
the simplest kind of lesson—
from a fruit jar cover!

My first turn was wrong;
but I was stubborn,
and I was strong.

The second was more wrong
because I was strong.

And now it sticks.

How sad to be strong
(and stubborn)
when you're wrong.

CONSOLED

He was a very little boy
who didn't want to move.
To leave his North Dakota friends,
his haunts, and hiding places
for Iowa fields and things and people
he hadn't seen before? Never!

He wouldn't be consoled.

They moved, and wonder of wonders,
a discovery: The moon had moved, too!
What consolation to find one familiar
    thing
to keep his world from crumbling!

What a pleasure to say,
"My moon, my sun,
my star and clouds and sky"
and know that all the while
I don't steal any of these from you!
But best of all, in our large moves,
God hears my cry and yours,
"My Lord, my Shepherd!"
In all our moving, this keeps us
right at home.

NATIVITY

I visited my friend today.
He's eighty-five
and travels light,
a wise and wonderful man.

We spoke of many things,
small talk and big talk,
and then he said,
"Yes, for most of our
comings and goings
maps are O.K.,
but for the Big Trip
we still follow the Star!"

Thanks to you, elder brother,
wanderer in my wilderness,
man of faith and vision.
You keep Christmas
in my heart.

THE STORY

What then shall this child be?

Luke 1:66

Births,
not bombs,
write the story.

Not footprints
in the sands,
but faithprints
in all lands.

SATISFIED

He commanded, he gave thanks, he
    blessed,
and the multitude ate that day.

I may not see the thousands fed
from one boy's dinner bag,
but I see morning dew on glistening grass
and walk in golden wind-waved fields.

My summer turns to autumn,
then hurries toward the winter rest,
but whether in sandwich or sacrament,
I meet the Christ
who asks me to look beyond my plate,
beyond the cup and chalice,
into that Face, and be at peace.